The Author

Joe Salazar holds a B.S. in Health Science and a J. D. in Law. He started four Martial Art schools, a software company, and a tax & accounting business. He has taught Bookkeeping, Accounting, and Income Tax classes, using both manual and computerized methods since 1984.

Before You Begin

This is written assuming the reader is in need of a review to assure competency with all arithmetic operations, so if you are not doubtful about addition, subtraction, multiplication, or division, then you need not review them. You should also be familiar with fractions and percentages. An introduction to Algebra is also helpful.

Often one will take a job or start a business thinking that writing letters, giving a good sales talk, and answering the phone are all that is required. The front office person is often surprised to be assigned a task involving some calculations.

The Bookkeeper or Accountant will prepare the Financial Reports. Accurate and timely information is needed to calculate budgets, advertising, payroll, income, and expenses for current and future tax periods. You may be asked to provide this information.

Hopefully, this small book will help you gain the knowledge that will lead to a successful career in business.

The following instructions, examples, and problems are some of those used in everyday business transactions. Results of calculations may differ by as much as 1% because of rounding error with different calculators.

When a computer or calculator is not available, you are expected to be able to conduct business as usual. Whether working for yourself or an employer, a math mistake is unacceptable and may be costly.

Lesson 1

Arithmetic & Fractions

Let us review some rules. "6/2" or "6÷2", means 6 divided by 2, "6(2)" or "6x2", means 6 multiplied by 2, "6-2" means 6 minus 2, and "6+2" means 6 plus 2.

The order of operations is always left to right in order.

8-1+3 is 8-1=7; 7 +3 = 10 **not 3+1=4; 4+8 = 12**

To find an average value; all values are added together then the total is divided by the number of values.

Example: Find the average of 22, 48, 17, and 65?

22 + 48 + 17 + 65 = 152   152 ÷ 4 = 38

Answer; the average is **38**

When we see a fraction we are looking at a number or symbol divided by another number or symbol. The top number or symbol, is called the *numerator* and the bottom number or symbol, is called the *denominator*.

One over 2, like this, ½, may be read as "one half", but is actually one divided by 2. The numerator, (1), is divided by the denominator, (2). This is true for all expressions written as a fraction.

Here's another way to look at fractions.

The numerator says how many parts to consider, out of the total parts shown by the denominator.

Example: ¾; a whole is divided into 4 parts and 3 of those parts are being considered.

Fractions may be added and subtracted when they have a common denominator.

Example: ¼ + ¾   = 4/4   = 1

When adding fractions with different denominators, a common denominator must be found.

Example: 3/5 + 6/15. Is there a number that both denominators are a multiple of? Yes, **5**.

1 times **5** = 5 and 3 times **5** = 15, so what can be done to make both denominators the same?   The denominator "5" when multiplied by 3 will equal"15". A fraction will not change

in value when the numerator and denominator are both multiplied or divided by the same number. Multiplying the numerator also by 3, 3/5 is converted to 9/15.

The fractions can now be added together to get the sum of; 9/15 + 6/15 =15/15 =1 or subtracted, 9/15 – 6/15 = 3/15 and the resulting fraction can be reduced by dividing both numerator and denominator by **3**, so 3÷**3** =1 and 15÷**3** = 5, therefore 3/15 = 1/5.

Am I right or wrong?

4/5 + 3/20 =	19/20
3/81 + 4/9 =	39/81
5/14 + 3/7 =	11/14
5/8 – 3/16 =	7/16

Test Yourself:

4/6 + 9/16 + 6/12 =

3/8 – 1/4 + 4/5 =

Fractions may be multiplied and divided. All numbers and symbols in an expression are assumed to have an unwritten denominator of 1. To multiply ¾ by 2 is the same as ¾ times 2/1. Here, 2 times 3 is 6, and 1 times 4 is 4, so we get 6/4 which may be reduced by, dividing by 2, to 3/2 = 1½. What if the denominator is not 1? Then multiply the top numbers by each other to get the solution numerator and the bottom numbers by each other to get the solution denominator.

Example: 6/7 x 3/9; 6x3=**18** and 7x9=**63**; solution=**18/63**

To divide one fraction by another, *invert the divisor and multiply.*

Example: 5/8 ÷ **4/5**   5/8 x **5/4** = 25/32

Am I right or wrong?

4/5 x 1/4 =	4/20 = 1/5
6/8 x ½ =	6/16 = 3/8
16/21 x 1/8 =	16/168 = 2/21
5/18 x 2/10 =	10/180 = 1/18
5/16 ÷ 3/5 =	25/48
3/5 ÷ ¼ =	12/5 = 2$2/5$

For mixed numbers, that is a whole number and a fraction, convert the whole number to a fraction then proceed.

Example: 3¼ x 3/5

    (a)   How many fourths in 3? 3 x 4 =12

    (b)   Add the numerator of the fraction; 12/4 + ¼ =13/4

    (c)   Now we can solve the problem. 13/4 x 3/5 = 39/20

    (d)   Reduce the fraction, 39/20 = $1_{19/20}$

Am I right or wrong?

3 ½ + ½ =	4.0
3 x 1/4 -1/4 + 7 =	$7_{1/2}$
5 x -3 + 1/3 =	$-14_{2/3}$
6/7 ÷ 5/4 =	24/35

Test yourself:

4/5 x 8 ÷ 2/3 + (2½)

Lesson 2

The Decimal

Remember the decimal places to the right of the decimal point: tents, hundredth, thousandths, ten-thousandths, etc.

When dealing with business matters, especially money, it is more convenient to convert fractions to their decimal form.

The decimal form of a fraction is found by identifying a factor that can be multiplied by the denominator to make it 100. This can be done by dividing 100 by the denominator.

Multiply both top and bottom numbers by that factor. The result is in hundredths and may now be written in the decimal form.

Example: $6/25 = 24/100 = .24$

To change a decimal to a fraction equivalent, write the decimal in the fraction form then reduce the fraction.

Example: $.08 = 8/100 = 2/25$

Am I right or wrong?

$4/5 =$ .80

$3/25 =$ .12

7/8 =	.875
.66 =	33/50
2/5 + .25 =	13/20
8/16 ÷ .50 =	1
3/5 - .2 + ½ =	.9
5 ½ x 4.2 + 1 =	24.1
4 x .25 – 1 =	0

Test yourself:

4/7 + 2/5 - .25 =

Lesson 3

Parentheses

When certain variables pertain only to certain parts of a problem, they may be grouped inside parentheses.

Example: $(2/3 - 1/3) \times (4/5 \div 5/8) = (1/3) \times (32/25) = 32/75$

When parentheses are present, the x meaning multiply, is understood.

Example: $(2/3 - 1/3)(4/5 \div 5/8) = 1/3(32/25) = 32/75$

To evaluate a complex math problem, 1st do all operations found in parentheses. Do the innermost parentheses first. 2nd do all multiplication and division from left to right. 3rd Add and subtract from left to right.

Example: $3 + 4 (6 / 2 (\mathbf{10 / 2})) - 4$

The innermost parentheses first 10 is divided by 2 then you have $3 + 4 (\mathbf{6/2(5)}) - 4$, next from left to right within the parentheses, $6/2 = 3$, leaving $3 + 4 (\mathbf{3 (5)}) - 4$, next $3 \times 5 = 15$ leaving, $3 + \mathbf{4 (15)} - 4$, and then you *dispose of the remaining parentheses by* $4(\mathbf{15}) = 60$, leaving you with, $\mathbf{3 + 60 - 4}$, only addition and subtraction to complete. $3 + 60 - 4 = \mathbf{59}$

Remember:

A minus times a minus = a plus, a minus times a plus = a minus, and a plus times a plus = a plus

Example: - 4 (-3) = 12   -4 (3) = -12   4 (3) = 12

Am I right or wrong?

3 (45 - 15) 2 =____   180

5 / 2 (18 + 6 - 20) + 1.5 =____   61.5

(4 + 17) - (15 / 3) =____   16

(9 -6) (9-6) = ____   9

24/3 (12 /4(5-3) (5/2.5) + 6) = ____   102

(100 / 25 / 5) 2 = ____   1.6

20+10/15/3(6+4) -12= ____   10.22

22 / (11(4+7)) +1 = ____   1.18

Test yourself: 5(-4(3/5) + 60) + 1 =

Lesson 4

Exponents

A number is raised to a power by multiplying it by itself. This is called a *power* and is written as a superscript to the right of the number being raised it is called an *exponent.* "2 squared" is written as 2^2, "2 cubed" is 2^3, "2 to the fourth power" is 2^4, and so on.

All numbers, symbols and expressions are assumed to have an unwritten exponent of 1 i.e. 9^1, R^1, $(A - 3)^1$

When a quantity is raised to a power the exponent is to the right of the quantity.

Example: $((2 + 6) / 4)^3 = (8/4)^3 = 2^3 = 2\,(2)\,(2) \quad = 8$

Another example is $5^4 = 5\,(5)\,(5)\,(5) \quad = 625$

Am I right or wrong?

$3^2\,(4^2 / 8) + 6 =$ _____ 　　　　　　　　24

$(3^3 / 9)^2 =$ _____ 　　　　　　　　9

$(3 + 4)\,(3 + 4^2) / 7 =$ _____ 　　　　19

$1^4(25 / 5) - 1 =$ _____ 　　　　　　　4

Test yourself:

$2^3 - 3 + 4^2 \div 21 =$

    Exponents with the same base can be added when multiplying or subtracted when dividing.

Example: $2^2 (2^2) = 2^4$ $3^5 / 3^3 = 3^2$ $4^{-5} (4^7) = 4^2$

Am I right or wrong?

$4^3 (3^2 / 3)(4^2)^2 =$ $4^3 (3)(4^4)$

$(5^3 \div 5^2)(3^2 - 4) =$ 25

$(12 - 10)^2 (22 - 5^2) =$ -12

$3 (3 + 4(3^2 \div 9)^2) =$ 21

Lesson 5

The Unknown Quantity

In Algebra letters may be used to represent numerals, this allows for generalized equations. For example; A + B = C. If C is 27 then A may equal any number from 0 to 27, while B may be 0 to 27, any combination that when added together may yield the desired result. In this case 0 + 27, 1 + 26, 25 +2, and so on.

Test Yourself:

If A +5 = 25 then what is A?

If an arithmetic operation is done to both sides of the equation the equation is still valid. The operation that will put the unknown quantity by itself on one side of the equation is the first step in identifying the unknown.

Consider A + 5 = 25. Subtracting 5 from A + 5 we get A, subtracting 5 from 25 we get 20, thus A =**20**.

The result is proven by substituting our result for the letter or symbol in the original expression; **20** + 5 = 25.

Look at 3 multiplied by A.

3 A = 12 may be treated this way. Divide both sides by 3.

3 A / 3 = 12/3 such that A = 4

We are using only positive numbers, but there are equations such as; minus 250 + B = 270, or A + 9 = - 10.

Am I Right or wrong?

A + 8 / 4 = 4	A = 2
B / 10 = 1.7	B = 17

When a number or another symbol, is written next to a symbol, it is implied that they are multiplied.

Am I right or wrong?

$(A^6 / A^2) (B^3 B^2) =$ _____	$A^4 B^5$
$B^3 - 26 = 1$ $B =$ _____	3
$(C C^2) (C^3 / C) =$ _____	C^5

The *distributive axiom* says that when a variable is multiplied by a quantity in parentheses, it may be distributed to all quantities and variables within the parentheses. Let's look at B (3+4), by distribution we have (3B + 4B) = 7B.

Now look at another equation, B $(B^2 - 5)$ = $(B^3 - 5B)$. The exponent of a quantity in parentheses is also distributed.

Example: $((3C) + C^2)^2 = ((3C)^2 + C^4) = 3^2C^2 + C^4$

If C=3 then: 9 x 9 + 81 = 9 x 9 + 81 = 162

Test yourself: A $(3^2 - 4)$ + 3A = 10;   A=

Finding the root can also be used to solve some equations.

Example: $C^3 - 13 = 14$.

Adding 13 to both sides gives

$C^3 - 13 + 13$ = 14 +13 = C^3 = 27

Taking the cube root on both sides gives us

$\sqrt[3]{C^3}$ = C and $\sqrt[3]{27}$ = 3   therefore; C =3

This type of problem seldom occurs in business calculations, except in building and construction.

Another method of solving complex equations for an unknown is to move everything to one side, making the other side zero!

Example: $3C^2 - 6(C^2) = 12$; subtracting 12 from both sides

$3C^2 - 6(C^2) - 12 = 0$; $3C^2 - 12 = 0$; $3C^2 = 12$; dividing by 3 we have $C^2 = 4$; $\sqrt[2]{C^2} = \sqrt[2]{4}$; $C = 2$

Test Yourself:

$3/5 \div (A-1)^2 = 15$ $\qquad\qquad$ A=?

Lesson 6

Percents

To find what percent one number (A) is of another number (B); 100% is divided by B and the result is multiplied by A

Example; 30 is what percent of 50? $100\% \div 50 = 2\%$

$2\% \times 30 = 60\%$

Answer; **30 is 60% of 50**

Am I right or wrong?

$20 = $ ___ % of 200	10%
$130 = $ ___ % of 650	19.5%
$1.65 = $ ___ % of 5	33%

Test Yourself:

$C - 6\%$ of $A = 30$. If $A = 100$ then $C = $ ___ ?

To raise A by a certain percent write the percent as a decimal equivalent then multiply A by **1 plus the decimal equivalent.**

Example: Raise $25 by 18%   18% = .18   25 x **1.18** = 29.50

Answer; raising $25 by 18% equals **$29.50**

Am I right or wrong?

9.90 + 10% =   10.89

450 + 15% =   517.50

Lowering a number "N1" by a stated percent, let's say n%, requires first to find 1 % of the number; N1/100. Then multiply by the percent to be subtracted; N2 = N1- (**n (N1/100)**)

250 – 5% = 250-(5(250/100)) = 250 – (5 (2.5)) = 250 – 12.50

250 -12.50 = <u>237.50</u> **or** 250 x .05 = 12.50; 250-12.50=<u>237.50</u>

To change a fraction to a percent; divide the denominator by **100%** then multiply the result by the numerator.

Example: change 4/5 to a percent   4/5 =? %

100% / 5 = 20%   20% x 4 = 80%

Answer; 4/5 = **80%**

Lesson 7

Probability

The chances of an event occurring is determined by calculating the *probability*. 100% is divided by the number of possibilities to find the percent of probability that one possible event may occur. If one of 4 possible events has the same chance, then 100% is divided by 4 to get 25%. If, from historical data, it is known that some events are more likely to occur than others; a different method is used.

We will say; retail goods have been shipped by train 50 times; 4 times goods were lost, 40 times goods arrived as scheduled, 1 time goods arrived late. And 5 times goods arrived early.

Here we divide 100% by the total events in history and multiply by the number of times each event occurred.

50 shipments	100% ÷ 50 =	2%
Lost	4	8%
As scheduled	40	80%
Late	1	2%
Early	5	10%

From this table we see that the chances of a shipment being lost are 8% and late 2% when shipped by train.

If lost and late are not acceptable, then adding the percentages tells us the method of shipping is 90% efficient.

Each method of shipping may be analyzed to find the most efficient one the budget can afford for the next 50 shipments.

Transporter	Efficiency	Cost	Lost & Late	Impact
Train	90%	$25,000	10%	-$2,500
Truck	82%	$20,000	18%	-$3,600
Air	96%	$32,000	4%	-$1,280

From this history we see that Air is the most efficient for on-time delivery, however; the company must determine if the cost is justified.

This is a matter for the financial accountant and company executives.

Am I right or wrong?

A rancher has 5 bulls and 1 cow the cow will have a calf in the spring.

The probability that any of the bulls is the sire is _____ 20%

Several bags of beans are received by a cannery. 12 bags have 600 beans, 8 bags have 750, and 30 bags have 650. The probability that the next bag will have more than 600 beans is_____   76%

XYZ corporation stock has this price track record for the last 6 months; Jan. 5.80, Feb. 6.20, Mar. 7.00, Apr. 7.10, May 7.10, and Jun. 7.50. The probability of the price going up more than 5% in July is _____   40%

Sometimes the need arises to find the probability that more than one event will occur at the same time. Is the most likely customer a man or a woman, and will that customer want brown or black boots?

HTB has sold 40 pairs of boots to women 25 pairs were brown and 15 pairs were black. They also sold 50 pairs of brown boots to men and 10 pairs of black. For restocking, HTB wants to order the boots that are most likely to sell.

The plan is to order 300 pairs. Should they order black or brown, for men or women? The table below is created.

	Men	Women
Black	10	15
Brown	50	25

Total	60	35

Total pairs sold = 100   100 =100% of boots sold

	Men	Women
Black	10%	15%
Brown	50%	25%

So the order for 300 pairs will consist of

	Men	Women
Black	30	45
Brown	150	75

Test yourself:

With this history, write an order for 180 pairs of boots, rounding to the nearest whole pair.

Lesson 8

A Service Business

Businesses need to know whether they are making a profit or taking a loss. Profit or loss is the difference between income and expenses.
They also need to be able to plan for the future by calculating the future cost of doing business.

The remaining lessons of this text will focus on the calculations needed to run a service business, a retail business, a manufacturing business, and payroll.

A service business does not sell property; they sell time, knowledge, and quality of work.

A retail business sells service and goods of some kind. They usually buy at wholesale prices and sell at retail or market prices.

A manufacturing business involves all of the above and buys or makes components to be assembled into a finished product or part for a product.

All businesses need to know how to process payroll if an employee is hired.

Let us start with rent. When a business space is rented to set up a business, it usually requires a lease for a stated number of years. Some landlords want the first and last month paid before the tenant may move in and take possession. The first month of rent is an *expense*. The last month of rent paid at the beginning of the lease is not an expense until the last month begins. Until then it is an *asset*.

An *Asset* is something owned an *Expense* is something purchased that costs less than $100 or has a useful life of one year or less.

If a security and/or utilities deposit is required, that too is an asset until used.

Repairs and painting are expenses; carpeting is an asset.

Any improvements to the leased space must be approved by the landlord. If the improvements are permanent, they belong to the property owner at the end of the lease, even if the tenant pays for them!

Current Assets are things owned that will lose all of their business value in one year or less. *Fixed Assets* are business items that will last more than a year and cost more than $100.

Starr Lite wants to open a boot cleaning & shining service for cowboys in the town of Horse Jaw. She finds a space that rents for $190 a month. She pays the first and last month in advance and a $175 security deposit. She buys a bucket of paint for $22.47, a broom for $6.99 and a shoe & boot shining kit for $33.64.

(1) What are her total assets?

(2) What are her total expenses?

Miss Lite opens a business checking account and deposits $5,000.00 in the account. The business checking account is a *Current Asset*. She then buys a large sign for the front window of her space to advertise her business and pays with a check. The sign costs $400.00 and will last for 7 years.

(3) What are her assets now?

The first month of business there are ten customers who have come in every week to get their boots cleaned and shined. Starr has this record.

Customer	Billed	Paid
Adams	40.00	15.00
Bonnie	120.00	100.00
Custer	75.00	75.00
Donner	22.50	22.50

Elko	114.00	
Fernandez	65.00	45.00
Gilligan	75.00	25.00
Henderson	100.00	100.00
Indio	79.85	37.63

(4) What is the total billed?

(5) What is the total paid?

(6) How much is owed to Miss Lite?

When a customer does not pay the whole balance due at the time of sale, the amount unpaid is called a receivable. *Accounts Receivable* is a Current Asset.

To find the average daily sales income for the 30 day month the owner will divide the total monthly sales by the number of days in the month.

(7) Compute the average daily sales.

To determine the percentage of customers who pay in full at the time of sale, divide the number of cash customers by the total number of customers, then multiply by 100%.

(8) What percent of the customers pay cash?

To find out what percent of amounts billed have been paid, divide the amount paid by the amount billed and multiply by 100%.

(9) What percentage of amounts billed have been paid?

Income from all sales has been deposited in the checking account.

(10) See if you can determine what percent of the checking account balance is due to sales income.

The break-even point for Starr is when she makes enough money to replace the money that was put into the business.

(11) How much more does Miss Lite have to make to break-even?

Test yourself: How much is the average sale per customer?

Lesson 9

A Retail Business

After a year in business Miss Starr Lite has done so well, she decides to begin a retail boot store. She gives notice to her current landlord that she will be moving to a larger space.

The new store opens on December, 1st. The store name is "Heel to Toe Boots" (HTB).

350 pairs of Tony Tiger boots are ordered by phone and charged to HTB's credit card.

Retail businesses buy goods at *wholesale prices* and sell at *market prices*.

The cost of the order is $21,000.

(12) What is the wholesale cost for one pair?

The credit card company interest is 18.24% of the outstanding balance per month. There are no other purchases on this card.

(13) What will be the amount of interest in 30 days?

(14) The credit card interest is added to the cost of the order to get a total of_____?

When this total is divided by the number of pairs you will get the actual expense for one pair of boots. Now Miss Lite decides the mark-up, to arrive at the market price. The boots are marked up 80% from the total cost; that is the cost per pair of boots is multiplied by 1.80 to get the retail or market price.

(15) How much is HTB selling a pair of boots for?

A person from Notches Gun Dealers calls to say "Valdez is coming" he will want two pairs of boots. Sales tax is 8% of the purchase price; Valdez gets 20% off the price of the second pair of boots.

(16) Prepare a receipt for this sale showing the discount and sales tax.

When a loan is made by a bank, simple interest is, in this case, 4.16%. After calculating the interest it is added to the principal. The total principal and interest is then divided by the number of payments. Starr Lite barrows $30,000 from the River Bank and will make 52 equal monthly payments.

(17) What will be the monthly payment?

Of 350 pairs of boots 275 pairs have been sold. To find the value of the remaining inventory the wholesale price is multiplied by the number of items held. (Exclude credit card interest)

(18) What is the value of the remaining inventory?

Because of the cost of doing business the retail price of boots is raised. The boots remaining in inventory are marked up another 5%.

A *casualty loss* of inventory is recovered at the market value.

(19) If the inventory is destroyed by fire, what is the loss to be claimed from the insurance company?

With business growing everyday an employee is hired as a floor salesperson. The rate of pay is $10.50 an hour plus 10% commission on all sales.

Gross Earnings is all earned wages before withholding taxes.

The employee, "Hank Curchiff" works 39 regular hours in a week and sells 12 pairs of boots.

(20) How much is Hank's gross earnings?

When Hank works more than 8 hours in a day or more than 40 hours in a week (Sun to Sat), he earns time and a half for the extra hours (overtime). Holiday hours pay double time.

This is Hank's time card for the first week in July.

DAY	Sun	Mon	Tue	Wed	Thu	Fri	Sat
DATE	2	3	4	5	6	7	8
Time in		9:00	9:00	9:00	9:00	9:00	9:00
Time out		6:00	6:00	7:00	6:00	8:00	11:00
Reg. Hrs.		8		8	8	8	
1.5 OT Hrs.				1		2	2
2.0 OT Hrs.			8				

These are his commission sales.

Sales	$40.00	$120.00	$65.80	$93.97	$315.25	$278.95
	Mon	Tue	Wed	Thu	Fri	Sat

(21) What are Hank's gross earnings for this week?

The actual payroll deductions and expense information varies by state, tax filing status, and other factors, but here you may use the following.

From The gross earnings there are these deductions, and these Employer expenses:

From Employee Earnings		Employer Tax Expense	
Federal Income Tax	17%		IRS
State Income Tax	6.2%		State
State Disability	2%		State
Social Security	6.5%	6.5%	SSA
Medicare	3.5%	3.5%	SSA
Unemployment Insurance		1.5%	State

(22) What is the amount of Hank's paycheck?

(23) What is the total payroll expense?

Test Yourself: Hank sold what percent more on Friday than he did on Monday?

Lesson 10

A Manufacturing Business

Miss Starr Lite finds a supplier who can furnish the parts and machinery to make boots for $5.25 each, so she decides to manufacture them rather than buy them.

The machinery will cost $12,000 installed. The body of the boot will cost $4.00 each, and the heel is $1.25 each.

The boot parts are *inventory parts*, the machinery is a *fixed asset*.

(24) If a pair of boots sells for $125.95 how many pairs need to be sold to pay for the parts and machinery? (Round up to the nearest pair)

The business is putting out 30 pairs a day, but needs to increase output by 20%.

(25) What will be 30 increased by 20%?

Fixed assets are not considered an expense at the time they are acquired; the cost is recovered by expensing them over time. This is called *depreciation.*

When equipment is no longer useful in a business, it still has some scrap value. This is called *Salvage Value.*

Basis is cost minus *accumulated depreciation.* Of course the first year accumulated depreciation is zero. Depreciation will accumulate until the cost is recovered. Each year accumulated depreciation increases and basis decreases by the same amount.

Depreciation Methods:

Straight Line

(Basis – salvage value) / Useful life = annual depreciation

Units of Output

(Units completed / Units expected) 100% = percent of depreciation

(Basis – salvage value) (% of depreciation) = current year depreciation

Working Hours

(Hours worked / Hours expected) 100% = percent of depreciation

(Basis – salvage value) (% of depreciation) = current year depreciation

Sum of the Years Digits

A fraction is created: The years of life remaining is the numerator.

The sum of the digits of the Useful life is the denominator.

Example: cost $1000   Salvage Value $20   Useful Life 5 years

First year of depreciation is calculated as;

(Cost – Salvage Value) (Useful life /Sum of the Years digits)

($1000-$20   )   (5   / (5 + 4 +3 +2 +1) or 15))

(980   )   (5   /   15)   = $326.67

Second year of depreciation fraction is 4 /15, third year is 3/15, and fourth year is 2/15. The final year is 1 /15. Thus 15/15 of the available depreciation has been completed.

Double Declining Balance

This method does not deduct salvage value.

100 % is divided by years of Useful Life remaining, and then the result is multiplied by 2. The result then is the percentage for depreciation.

Example: cost $9,578   Useful Life 5 years

100% ÷ 5 years = 20%   20% (2) = 40%   .40 ($9,578)

= $3,831.20 First year depreciation

Let us say we have a machine costing $29,483.96 with a useful life of 12 years. This machine will run for 35,500 hours and in that time it will put out 55,000 units. Salvage value is $2,500.

So far, we have put out 20,250 units in 6,228 hours.

(26) Calculate the first year's depreciation with each method.

Test Yourself: Depreciate your family car by each method; a car's life time output is a hundred thousand miles and it has a life of 5 years.

If a company sells stock, the investor who buys the stock expects a profit when the shares are sold to another investor, broker or back to the company. Stock value changes with what the buyers are willing to pay for a share.

Many public projects are supported by bond sales; a bond is usually purchased and sold at a predefined price. Since the bond has a sure cash-in value, the bond is a safer investment.

Stock may be more risky, but may yield a greater percent of profit in a shorter time. The investor must always weigh the risk against the potential profit.

Investments are assets until cashed out. When cashed out, an investment may yield a profit or a loss.

Starr Light bought 100 shares of Toe Nails, Inc. at $6.50 a share. Building in Horse Jaw is booming; 10,000 new homes will be in place within the year. Homes are held together with nails, so Starr's stock has gone up 60% in value. Her sister Moon tells her to sell the stock and buy bonds with the proceeds. Since Moon Lite is brighter than Starr Lite, Starr considers it. The recommended bond costs $9.20 and at maturity, may be redeemed for $15.00.

(27) How many bonds can Starr buy with the proceeds? (Round down to the nearest whole bond)

(28) What percent increase will the bonds yield over the price?

Starr decides to stick with the stock market and buys 500 more shares at the current price.

(29) How much does she pay?

The list or records of one's investments is called a *portfolio*.

(30) What is the value of Miss Lite's portfolio?

Test Yourself: How much has the investment made so far?

Lesson 11

Business Practice

Hank starts his own Auto Repair business; he finds an old garage building that rents for $2,000 a month. He pays the first and last month in advance and a $1,000 security deposit. Cash that might be used at any time is always a current asset.

He buys a complete set of auto mechanic hand tools for $15,000 that will last 20 years and then he can sell them for $100. License and permits cost him $580, a hydraulic car lift is installed for $27,893 and will be a permanent fixture.

The cost of the lift will be *amortized* over 7 years that means the same as straight line depreciation with no salvage value because, if Hank moves, he can't take it with him. Every year, for 7 years, the equipment is used he will take a deduction for one seventh of the cost and his basis will decrease accordingly. If he must move sooner, he will deduct the remaining amount in the year of the move.

(31) What are his total assets?

(32) What are his total expenses?

Hank opens a business checking account and deposits $120,000.00 in the account. He then buys a sign billboard for the roof to advertise his business and pays with a check for $2,500. The sign will last for 10 years and then it will be worth only $50.

(33) What will be his total business assets after one year of straight line depreciation and amortization?

The first week there are 20 customers. The sales tax rate is 8.2%; his labor charge is $53 an hour.

Job	Parts	Tax	Hours	Labor	Total Billed
New Tires	524.65	$	.5	$	$
Used Tires	240.00		.5		
Front Brakes	140.00		1		
Rear Brakes	150.00		1.2		
Trans, Install	375.84		3.5		
Lube & Oil	13.50		.25		
Fix Flat	1.20		.15		
Headlts Rewire	7.22		2.5		
Fend, Repair Dent	4.35		3.4		

(34) Complete the sales summary for the week.

A customer died and his family told Hank they would not drive the car that was left in the shop. They told him to keep the car as payment for the repair bill of $1,625. The car's book value is $6,000. Any money, more than the bill, is gift or gratuity income and is taxable.

(35) At a rate of 22%, how much is the tax on the gift income?

(36) What percent of the sales is due to New Tires?

(37) If the new tires cost $8.43 wholesale and sell for $45.27 retail, how much profit is made on 16 new tires?

(38) Employees' earnings are reported on Form W-2 and non employee compensation is reported on Form 1099 Misc. If reports are required for non employee compensation of more than $600, how many hours will that be at $12.00 an hour?

Hank uses his mobile phone for both business and personal calls; he made 210 personal calls and 522 business calls. He pays 28 cents a call. His phone bill is $204.96.

(39) What amount is deductible as a business expense?

Hank uses his personal car as a loaner to his customer. His commuting miles driven are 8,345 and loaner miles are 84. The total miles driven are 12, 595.

(40) How many other personal miles are driven?

(41) At 55 cents a mile, what is the business expense?

Depreciation is straight line for 5 years but only for the portion that is business related.

(42) Hank's basis in the car is $29,000. A car's salvage value is $500. Calculate the first year of annual depreciation and determine the business part.

Test Yourself: A party host spills grape juice on a woman's gown the gown depreciates at $912.00 a year for 4 years, then will be worth only $2. She bought it 3 years and 1 day ago for $3,650.

If she sues the host for the *value at the time of damage*; how much could she recover?

A hospital ward requires 4 staff on the floor at all times. Each employee may not work more than 40 hours in a seven day week; lunch break not included. Employees are not paid for their 30 minute lunch breaks. How many employees are needed? (Round up to the nearest whole person)

Hours in week = 24 hrs. (7 days) = 168 hrs *a hospital is a 24 hrs a day, 7 days a week business*

Lunch break   = .5 hr. (3 shifts) (7 days) = 10.5 hrs. *3 shifts' lunch breaks per week*

10.5 hrs + 168 hrs = 178.5 hours to cover the ward

178.5 hrs to cover / 40 hrs a week per person = 4.46 persons required   = **at least 5** persons needed

Test yourself: Are you able to create a 1 month work schedule for the hospital ward?

Remember everyone wants at least one week-end a month off!

Odds and Ends

Starr Lite buys a business insurance policy for $200 a year and prepays for 4 years. The policy is effective immediately.

(43) How much is an expense and how much is an asset?

Hank has an employee who worked 40 hours at $10.50/hour. The employee also worked for Starr as a non-employee at the same rate of pay for 70 hours.

(44) How much gross earnings is reported on a W-2 and how much is reported on a 1099 Misc?

While building his own house, Hank buys 10,000 6d nails from Toe Nail, Inc. he pays $3000. 16% of the nails are defective and hank returns them.

(45) What will be his refund?

Compound Interest is earned on some investments. The formula for determining the future value of such an investment is: **FV = P $(1 + r)^N$**

FV = future value   P = present value   r = rate of interest

N = number of years

Future value is, Present Value multiplied by (1 + rate of interest expressed as a decimal) with the part in parentheses being raised to the power of Years.

Example: $1000 invested for 2 years at 10%

Future Value = 1000 $(1 + .10)^2$ = 1000 (1.21) = 1,210

Hank invests $5000 for 3 years at 5%.

(46) What is the value of the investment in three years?

In the business of buying and selling food there are special considerations for aging, waste, spoilage and transportation. Fruits and vegetables lose quality with time from harvest to market. Animals are not completely consumed as human food; some parts are sold to pet food producers. Skins go to furniture and clothing factories.

Spoilage, in the case of perishables, means no longer "saleable". If the merchant cannot recover from the supplier, the cost of the non-saleable inventory may be added to the saleable inventory.

80 lbs. of tomatoes are purchased and paid for. Business is slower than expected and 10% are spoiled, and the supplier has gone out of business.

(47) If the cost of the tomatoes was $38.00, what is reported as spoilage loss?

(48) What was the cost of one pound of tomatoes before spoilage?

(49) What is the cost of one pound of tomatoes after spoilage?

In the business of gathering and processing natural resources there is *depletion* of the resource. The value of a mine or a well goes down as harvesting goes up.

The cost of land, options to explore, permits, equipment, and labor are weighed against the potential profits.

A piece of land costs $80,000. Equipment will be $35,000 and Labor will be $6,000 a day. Mining permits will cost $15,000. The land is expected to yield minerals with a value of $220,000 by the end of the 15th day of mining and be 100% depleted on day 16.

(50) Will it be worth starting this project?

A 900 lb. steer on-the-hoof sells for $1,200. Beef is selling for $1.05 a pound, wholesale, and $2.20 a pound, retail. The steer is 62% beef, by weight. The non-beef parts can be sold for $700 retail.

(51) Is there a retail profit in purchasing this steer?

Test Yourself: Medical school tuition is $65.000 a year, for 4 years.

A newly graduated doctor receives $800 a week as an intern. 75% of his income covers his living expenses. Paying 25% of his income to his student loan for tuition; how long will it take to pay the loan in full with 3.5% simple interest?

Concrete is ordered and sold by the cubic yard. The job specifications are converted to cubic yards and then the job cost is determined.

To find the area of any shape, the perimeter is measured and divided by 4. The result is squared to get the area.

$A = (p/4)^2$

An "s" shaped driveway is the job; it needs to be at least 2 inches thick.

Measurements are taken: Length 85 feet, Width 12 feet

All measurements are converted to a common unit

85' (12') (2") =   1,020" (144") (2") = 293,760 cubic inches

293,760 cubic inches ÷ 12 inches per foot = 24,480 cubic feet

24,480 cubic feet ÷ 3 feet per yard = 8,160 cubic yards

Or 293,760 cubic ~~inches~~ / 36 ~~inches~~ /yard = 8,160 cubic yards

(52) If the cost of concrete is $4.50 / yard^3 and labor is $33.75 / hour; what will be the cost to pour the driveway in 5 hours?

Specifications for a swimming pool are; 3 inches thick, 3 feet deep at the shallow end, 12 feet deep at the other end, constant slope from end to end, 50 feet long by 20 feet wide. The surface shape is rectangular.

First the length of the slope must be calculated by finding the Hypotenuse of a right triangle.

The length is one side (a); the deep end depth is another side (b). The hypotenuse or sloping bottom is the third side (H).

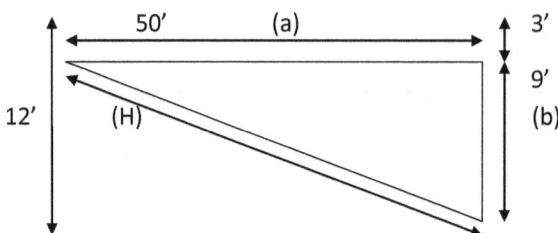

Where a level line, parallel to a side wall, from the bottom of the shallow end wall meets the deep end wall a right angle is formed.

The hypotenuse of a right triangle is the square root of the sum of the squares of the two adjacent sides. $H = \sqrt{a^2 + b^2}$

$H = \sqrt{50^2 + 9^2}$ $H = \sqrt{2,500 + 81}$ $H = \sqrt{2,581}$

H = 50.80 feet

50.80' x 20' x 3" = concrete for *bottom*   12,192 Yards^3

Sides: 3' + 50' + 12' + 50.80' = 115.8'   *perimeter of side*

115.8 ÷ 4 = 28.95' length and width *if side were square*

28.95^2 = 838.10 square feet *is the area of one side*

2 (838.10' x 3") = concrete *for 2 sides*   1,676.20 Yards^3

End Walls:

Shallow end 3' by 20' by 3"

3' x 20' x 3" = concrete for *shallow end wall*   720 yards^3

Deep end 12' by 20' by 3"

12' x 20' x 3" = concrete for *deep end wall*   2,880 Yards^3

Total   5,276.20 Cubic Yards of concrete

5,277 estimated cubic yards needed. Some concrete will always stick to surfaces of tools and containers.

For construction project materials estimates, round up the final total to the next whole number.

Labor requirements:

Backhoe rental, 8 hours @ $7.50/hr.

Backhoe Operator, 8 hours @ $13.65/hr.

Form Setting Crew, 4 workers, 8 hours @ $9.50/hr each.

Concrete delivery and pouring will be, 2 days 4 hours/day @ $10.50/hr.

Trowel ling and finishing crew, 2 workers 8 hours @ $12/hr each.

Form removal and touch up crew, 3 workers for 3 hours @ $9.50/ hr each.

Test yourself:

If concrete is delivered already mixed, and sells for $85/Yd^3; what will be the bill for this Olympic size pool?

Final Examination

Open Book

100% is passing!   Anything less is bad business!

1) Prepaid rent is

    A. An asset

    B. An expense

    C. Inventory

2) Assets are listed on

    A. The balance sheet

    B. The inventory

    C. The income statement

3) Merchandise held for sale is

    A. Profit

    B. Expense

    C. Inventory

4) The employer has no payroll expense other than wages

    True

    False

5) Liabilities is what is owed to the business

True

False

6) A business must pay all accounts receivable

True

False

7) Money used to purchase stock is

A. An expense

B. An investment

C. Neither

8) An investment is listed on the books as

A. A liability

B. An asset

C. An inventory item

9) 80% may be written as

A. .80

B. .08

C. 8.0

10) Cost recovery over time is called

A. Accounts payable

B. Asset allocation

C. Depreciation

11) After its usefulness to a business equipment will still have

A. Salvage value

B. Renewal value

C. Effective value

12) As accumulated depreciation increases basis

A. Remains the same

B. Decreases

C. Increases

13) 62% of $8,000 is

A. $49.60

B. $496.00

C. 4,960.00

14) To increase 300 by 6% multiply by

A. 1.6

B. 1.06

C. .16

15) The investment with the greater risk is

A. Bonds

B. Stock

16 Permanent improvements to business property belong to

A. The landlord

B. The tenant

17) The employee sends the payroll deductions to the government

True

False

18) Deposits for future use are

A. Assets

B. Liabilities

C. Expenses

19) For equipment costing $10,000, a salvage value of $500, and a life of 4 years, the method to take the most depreciation in the first year is

A. Straight line

B. Double declining balance

20) Depreciable business property costs at least ___ and lasts more than___

A. $25, and 13 months

B. $100, and 1 year

C. $1, and 1 year

Answers to lesson problems

(1)   Prepaid rent   190.00

Security Deposit   175.00

Total Assets   **265.00**

(2)   Rent   290.00

Paint   22.47

Broom   6.99

Shining Kit   33.64

Total Expenses   **253.10**

(3)   Carried forward   265.00

Bank Checking   4,600.00

Sign   400.00

Total Assets   **5,265.00**

(4)   **691.35**   **(5)**   **420.13**   **(6)**   **271.22**

(7)   691.35 / 30 = **23.05**   **(8)**   (3/10) = .3   .3 x 100 =30   **30%**

(9)   420.13 / 691.35 = .61   **61%**   **(10)**   4,600 + 420.13 = 5,020.13

420.13 / 5,020.13 = .08   = **8%**

(11)   5,618 – 420.13 = **5,197.97**   **(12)**   21,000 /350 = **60.00**

(13)   21,000 X .1824 = **3,830.40**   **(14)**   21,000 + 3,830.40 = **24,830.40**

(15)   24,830.40 /350 = 70.94   70.94 X 1.80 = **127.69**

(16)   127.69 X .20 = 25.54 off 2nd pair of boots

127.69 – 25.54 = 102.15

102.15 + 127.69   =   229.84 retail price

229.84 X .08   =   18.39 sales tax

229.84 + 18.39   =   **248.23**

(17)

Principal	Interest Rate	Interest	Term
30,000	4.16%	1,248	52 months
Total of payments 31,248		monthly payment **600.92**	

(18)   21,000 /350 = 60   350 – 275 = 75   75 X 60.00 = **4,500**

(19)   127.69 X 5% = 6.38   134.07 X 75 = **10,055.25**

(20)

Wages	Commission	Gross Earnings
10.50 X 39 = 409.50	275 X 10% = 27.50	**437.00**

(21)

Reg. Hrs.	32	336.00
1.5 OT Hrs.	5	393.75
2.0 OT Hrs.	8	168.00
Commissions		913.97
Gross Earnings	**1,811.72**	

(22)

From Employee Earnings

(23)

Employer Expense

Federal Income Tax	17%	307.99		
State Income Tax	6.2%	112.33		
State Disability	2%	36.23		
Social Security	6.5%	117.76	6.5%	117.76
Medicare	3.5%	63.41	3.5%	63.41
Unemployment			1.5%	27.18
Total Deductions		637.72		
Net Check	**1,174.00**		**Payroll Expense**	**1,811.72**

(24)

Parts = 5.25 X 2 = 10.50

125.95 – 10.50 = 115.45 profit on 1 pair of boots

12,000 / 115.45 = 103.94 = 104 pairs of boots to pay for machinery

104 X 10.50 = 1,092

12,000 + 1,092 = 13,092 Total cost of parts and machinery

13,092 / 115.45 = 113.4 = **114 pairs of boots**   114 X 115.45 = **13,161.30**

(25)

30 X .20 =6   30 + 6 = **36**

(26)

Straight Line: 29,483.96 – 2,500 = 26,983.96 to be depreciated over 12 years

26,983.96 / 12 = **2,248.66** annual depreciation

Units of Output: 20,250 / 55,000 = .37

26,983.96 X .37 = **9,984.07 =**   1st Yr. Depreciation.

Working Hours: 6,228 / 35,500 = .18

26,983.96 X .18 = **4,857.11=**   1st Yr. Depreciation.

Sum of the Years Digits: 12 / 74 = .16

26,983.96 X .16 = **4,317.43=**   1st Yr. Depreciation.

Double Declining Balance: 100% / 12 = 8.33% 2 X 8.33 = 16.66%

29,483.96 X .1666 = **4,912.03**= 1st Yr. Depreciation

(27) 100 X 6.50 = 650   650 x 1.6 = 1,040   1,040 / 9.20 = 113.04 = 113 **bonds**

(28) 15 - 9.20 = 5.80   5.80 / 920 X 100 = **63.04%**

(29) 6.50 X 1.6 =10.40   10.40 X 500 = **5,200**

(30) 600 shares @ 10.40 a share **= 6,240**

(31)   45,893.00   **(32)   2,580**   **(33)   160,918.29**

(34) Job	Parts	Tax	Hours	Labor	Total Billed
New Tires	524.65	**41.97**	.5	**26.50**	**593.12**
Used Tires	240.00	**19.68**	.5	**26.50**	**286.18**
Front Brakes	140.00	**11.48**	1	**53.00**	**204.48**
Rear Brakes	150.00	**12.30**	1.2	**63.60**	**225.90**
Trans, Install	375.84	**30.82**	3.5	**185.50**	**592.16**
Lube & Oil	13.50	**1.11**	.25	**13.25**	**27.86**
Fix Flat	1.20	**.10**	.15	**7.95**	**9.25**
Headlts Rewire	7.22	**.59**	2.5	**132.50**	**40.31**
Fend, Fix Dent	4.35	**.36**	3.4	**180.20**	**184.91**

(35) 962.50   **(36)** 27%   **(37)** 589.44   **(38)** 50

(39) 146.16   **(40)** 4,166   **(41)** 46.20   **(42)** 58.00

(43) 200 expense and 600 assets

(44) 420.00 on W2 and 735.00 on 1099

(45) 480.00   **(46)** $5000 (1.05)^3$ = 5000 X 1.16 = 5,800

(47) 3.80   **(48) 38 /40 = .95**   **(49) 38 / 36 = 1.06**

(50) 80,000 + 35,000 + 90,000 + 15,000 = 220,000   **No**

(51) 900 (.62) = 558 pounds of beef

2.20 – 1.05 = 1.15 retail profit per pound

1.15 (558) =641.70 retail potential for beef

641.70 + 700 = 1,341.70   **Yes**

(52) 36,720 concrete + 168.75 labor = **36,888.75**

Final Examination Answers

1.	A
2.	A
3.	C
4.	F
5.	F
6.	F
7.	B
8.	B
9.	A
10.	C
11.	A
12.	B
13.	C
14.	B
15.	B
16.	A
17.	F
18.	A
19.	B
20.	B

www.ingramcontent.com/pod-product-compliance
Lightning Source LLC
Chambersburg PA
CBHW071810170526
45167CB00003B/1253